New Grammy country song lyrics

Santiago Alexander "SANTI" Polito

authorHOUSE®

AuthorHouse™
1663 Liberty Drive
Bloomington, IN 47403
www.authorhouse.com
Phone: 833-262-8899

Published by AuthorHouse 04/27/2021

ISBN: 978-1-6655-2426-1 (sc)
ISBN: 978-1-6655-2425-4 (e)

Library of Congress Control Number: 2021908504

Print information available on the last page.

Genre Country Music

Grammy country song

With all my heart desires,
I wished you the best life.

You left me feeling immortal
after I got to know you and your friends
With all my feelings
I felt good to you and to nobody else.

When thinking about this party
with your family and friends,
I remember seeing you for the first time
at this person's house answering to your name.

You made it easy for me.
You let me be free
when I'm with you

I started to wonder
if we could be more than friends
and become a family.

Seeing you tonight—
February of 2021—
was the best feeling I've ever had
since you passed away

I still remember
picturing you and me together.
I wished a better life for you,
and your friends and family.

Mr. Santiago Alexander "SANTI" Polito is 40 years old and writes for Grammy award winner singers like Franco Deliz and many more. MR. Polito's work is not yet known to the public just yet but he's hoping to hit big when Franco Deliz told him his music is worth $1,000,000.00USD each song then he knew he was ready. From "Santi" thank you for buying my book, hopefully you'll enjoy it as much as Grammy singers enjoy their job.

Printed in the United States
by Baker & Taylor Publisher Services